The Tension Zone

The Tension Zone

by
Sarah Gorham

FOUR WAY BOOKS
Marshfield

Please direct inquiries to:
Editorial Office
Four Way Books
PO Box 607
Marshfield, MA 02050

Library of Congress Number: 95-61376

ISBN 1-884800-06-8

Cover painting by Susan Finnegan: "Refulgence." Used by permission of the artist.
Text design by Acme Art, Inc.
Cover design by The Creative Team
Manufactured in the United States of America.

This book is printed on acid- free paper.

Four Way Books is a division of Friends of Writers Inc.,
a Vermont-based not-for-profit organization.

Second printing. 1999

Jeffrey

ACKNOWLEDGMENTS

The American Voice: "Bisecting a Water Lily," "The Empress Calls on the Goddess of Mercy," "Dwarf Apricot"

Cincinnati Poetry Review: "Motherly and Auspicious," "The Empress and the Railroad," under the title "1900, Peking"

Grand Street: "The Minor Manchu's Daughter"

The Kenyon Review: "Concubine of the Lowest Rank," "Visit from the Footbinder," "Man Drinking a Cup of Coffee," "My Daughter Defaces the Life of Emily Dickinson"

The Louisville Review: "Stillborn," "Highway Marker, Route 71 Carrollton"

The Missouri Review: "Cautionary Tale, 3 AM," "Clear Air Turbulence," "Hot Water," "Water House, Shakertown," "Tiptoe," "The Tension Zone"

New Letters: "Oval"

North Atlantic Review: "Crossing Guard," "Extra Extra"

The Ohio Review: "National Enquirer"

Ploughshares: "The Empress Speaks to Buddha," "Moon Cakes"

Poetry: "Ode to the Intellect," under the title "Hymn to the Intellect"

Poetry Northwest: "Circles," "Starfish," "Snow Melt," "I Go Back"—Winners of the 1990 Carolyn Kizer Award

Sparrow: "The Dying Empress," "The Empress Receives the Head of a Taiping Rebel," "Ideogram (after Fenollosa)"

William and Mary Review: "Imperial Gown," "The Empress's Fan," "Last Request"

"Notes from a Chinese Love Manual—1. The White Tiger Leaps" and "The Empress Receives the Head of a Taiping Rebel" appeared in *A Formal Feeling Comes: Formal Poetry by North American Women,* edited by Annie Finch (Story Line Press, 1994).

The author wishes to thank the Kentucky State Arts Council, the Kentucky Foundation for Women, and the Corporation of Yaddo for their generous support.

CONTENTS

FOREWORD

This year two books split the prize in this Four Way Books competition — Stuart Friebert's *Funeral Pie* (a collection marked by unusual warmth and forthrightness, humor and a colloquial immediacy) and the book you have before you, Sarah Gorham's pattern-appointing, elegantly artful work *The Tension Zone.* I was lucky to be able to award both books the first place distinction (Four Way is a press with a taste for the eclectic). These two books remind us, despite rumors to the contrary, how varied and inventive American poetry remains.

Gorham's *The Tension Zone* will not easily be subsumed under any banner. Perhaps its most easily notable feature is the homage it pays to forms. By forms I mean not only literary forms — though a remarkable series of sonnets is woven through the book, concentrating on the life of the Chinese Empress Dowager. These sonnets contain elegant turns of perception and intellection, but frequently close with a ferocious power, like the jaw of a beautifully-furred predator. To say that they operate by a combination of mind and muscle might suggest some qualities of Gorham's literary powers. But through all the poems runs a love of forms even more fundamental: Gorham pays a constant close attention to the shapes of experience, the patterns which befall us in a physical world.

And her best poems attend to the forms of ideas. The physical geometries of "Surveyors" move "the search for exact value" through vectors of analog to "no place like home" and "someone's idea of hell." The bright nuggets of the poem "Casual Lies" are diamonds of insight, served to the sensual eye: even the tub of margarine and "the knife, inherited" serve as occasions — not (as is so common in contemporary American poems) for metaphor but, more iconoclastically, for metaphor's fundamental undermining. Gorham's intelligence is shot through with regard (a patient, naturalist's regard) for the shapes of organic life; the tension zone is the habitable margin, a natural boundary where "if you need someone to blame" you have nature's proliferations and predations to study, the angry red of the "cardinal under siege," and the "popped egg-sac / unfolding at your feet."

Gorham's sense of shapeliness informs the overall design of the collection, as well. Poems follow one on another in sympathies of shape: after the poem "Two Fish Eye-to-Eye" (a love manual's position), comes an account of a woman giving birth secretly, fearing the shame of having a girl; this poem closes "A boy and his mother easily advance. / A girl: two ghosts tied back-to-back." So the Janus-twin figures at the heart of the sexual act now incur the twisted figures of the ghosts of girls in China; such doublings and twists can't help deepening toward DNA. And we are prepared, by an intelligent pre-arrangement of image-relations, for the subtle inversions of the next poem, "Man Drinking a Cup of Coffee" (a poem that starts with a moon and some "dissolving grounds," moves to a lake and round black window, and ends with the form of an Ophelia that "surges down his throat, / her long dark dress spreading / into all his secret places"). The poem after THAT is entitled "Circles." Anyone inclined to understand the ways in which images mount and amount to meaning, from poem to poem, could study Gorham's sequencing to great advantage.

Toward the end of the book, a character sighs "*Make way for the image / of God*...then as usual / she reconsiders." Too few poets today would add the reconsideration. And the premises of all forms (and all love of form) become very much to the point, in the poem "Last Request" (Gorham's too smart to place this poem last in the book, but with it she astutely prepares us for the book's last turns, toward releasings of all that is held — not only breath, but ground and grudge as well). "The dead cannot shout... Build me a paper house crammed with money, paper lutes... Burn them all... Smoke is a kind of heavenly translator. / I cannot choke. / ...I'll bless your marriage bed. / Don't hesitate to ask / for more. Our need connects us. / It's freedom I dread." In the poem's last balancing of terms — connection and need, dread and freedom — we recognize the meaning of a mortal attachment to forms. Sarah Gorham administers her arts toward that rare end — the paradoxical snap when two crucial things come together — structural necessity and intellectual surprise — a convergence that nature has always made convincing.

—*Heather McHugh,* judge
Four Way Books
Award Series

Surveyors

The search for exact value
begins as two well-dressed men
splay their telescopes
and pin down the alley's cobbled
hypotenuse, unaware that

just below, a sewer rat
figures his own territory
running squares like a color-blind
Mondrian, medium brown
bead on an abacus.

Pretty kitty, the child purrs
and then returns to her own
channel of reassurance, pink
chalk vector running from hydrant
to sewer cap. Good to evil,

safe to sorry, she hops.
Hip hip I hear the men shout
or however their argot
runs—brick into numbers
stamped on a water blue sheet.

They pack up and scurry home,
but there's no place like home
that hasn't been bisected
at least once by animal or child
or someone's idea of hell too.

National Enquirer

A gun in a silver jacket. A small,
thin one to fit in the back
pocket of your jeans.
This is what you want today.

A gold and crimson convertible
just like the one on Q street,
its cool shadow across the Coke
machine, the glinty night.

The shock you felt when Jack
walked over. Close enough
to feel his breath, to guess
the metallic flavor of his mouth.

But do you
really want to know,
feel your longing wash up
against him, and finding no escape,

filter in to die?
Why then, they'd have to
hang a sign—*No Vacancy.*
And it's the vacancy you love,

the scent of the undiscovered
restaurant, a stranger waiting.
The crimes, the poetry you never
thought you were capable of.

Ode to the Intellect

When you are confused,
take the jacketed arm of thought.
His face has a violet pallor
and is, we imagine, immortal.
Thought noiselessly
feathers the sky, moves like a glider
over mountains where we've heard
survivors devoured the dead.
Only their jewelry remains.
Thought heals without stitches.
He floats through the hallways,
an IV tree with no
pretence of commitment,
no bedside manner.
Only rarely does his voice
arc into a steely falsetto.
And who cares for the lowly heartbeat?
Who remembers?
Cling to thought, and in time,
your friends will back away.
Betrayal is necessary—
even the lobby plant drops its leaves,
turns skinny in the dark. I promise
if you stand tall by his words,
if you utter and reutter his principles
there will be no bleeding,
no sap left to drip, no
weeping by the bathroom window.

Casual Lies

1. Diamond

Kilamanjaro of my
very own. Star
carried into this century
by a snail.

2. Anaesthesia

Relax. 99, 98, 97, 96 . . .
Think of sheep returning,
single file.
Only one stall left
with a back door,
the one you want.

3. Wolf

Wet fur spikes
like fins on an old Cadillac.
Eye an infrared slash.
Stalking the caribou, he's one
mean parallelogram.

4. Margarine

Her hands are birds of paradise.
The knife, inherited, spirals
down into the yellow tub.
The muffin blazes
like a queen's crown.

5. Excuse Me

Password of the dandelion,
skateboard, the insubordinate
sneeze. Their motto?
The only good view
is an empty one.

6. Obsession

It's only a scratch.
Or have you caught
destiny by the tail,
dark spiny thing, its head
thrashing in crimson waters?
Oh, hang on, do.
Just in case.

The Tension Zone

Concordia discors (Horace)

You have a home but not in the
aloof gallery of climax forest and not
in the meadow's quilted safety.
Come to the edge instead, the ecotone
where wood and field, cliff and stream
jag together, where snakeroot
flames into aspen and light
and shadow try a tense handshake, a sweaty mix
of daisy, moss, grasshopper, and slug.
This is life along the margin,
breath among the multitudes where twice
the species tumble in half the space.
A sparrow stretches its claim,
pushing with little jabs of sound
like hail on aluminum. A spider knits
double the web, jumps out like a rusty
claw. So if you are restless and cramped,
tired of the solitary fight under your
dark canopy of soul; if you need
someone to blame, come to the tension zone.
The enemy is here, and grows up and out
and looms, an extra long
Smilax tendril, a popped egg-sack
unfolding at your feet. Your fear
is only natural, the local tongue.
And anger flares into beauty
like the jittery switchblade
crest of a cardinal under siege.

Tiptoe

The Chinese claim
when a crocodile
staggers from the river
to swallow a dog,
another Buddha
enters
Nirvana. Perhaps
all earthly effort,
even the awkward kind,
has its heavenly
counterpart,
as up on our toes, reaching
for a box in some dark
little corner we are
climbing out of ourselves,
though it may
feel like greed,
like pride. This then
the mirror action of will:
in our height is
our smallness,
in our fall, grace.

Imperial Gown

It slipped from under the velvet
sedan, one sleeve, and she begged it all.
The dragon and the pearl of potential.
The silver-haired bat. The infinite
pattern of red-stitched truths.
How much of the emperor is kept from view!
So sweet to wear this kind
of flattery! But the day was a poor-coat day.
She picked up her jacket and cotton pantaloons.
They limped along her skin,
they sucked her legs. She swayed
into the sea of leggings—it was noon,
and she muttered: where's the man
could ease a heart like a yellow satin gown?

Visit from the Footbinder

Little shoes sell quickly in shop
windows. Three inch tracks peel
off garden sand. If too large, crop
or bandage your feet. Force heel
under instep to meet your bent
digits. Bind them like crescent
moons that peep into the night.
A mistress shouldn't stray. Slowly
she sways. She hovers and floats,
point dancer, Buddha on tiptoe.
Dab with your spirit, microscopic
drip by drip. As you walk, feel it
evaporate. Anything more is a lie.
There is no permanent I.

The Minor Manchu's Daughter

"I forget my father every moment.
I tear his banner into bird-sized rags
and throw them to the wind.
I have a coin he once gave me.
I tried to bring myself to spend it
but a beggar danced in my gut. He nagged
and nagged. As if I were his friend
he spouted his mediocre lines. He pleaded.
I forget my father every day.
In his grave. In his humble sandals
that shied away from mountains.
I set my heart on those mountains.
They are steep and rich and full
of change. I'll lose my mother along the way."

My Daughter Defaces the Life of Emily Dickinson

She carries the book upstairs,
showing me with a rough hand
what she's highlighted.
Not, I'm annoyed to see,
in see-through yellow
or orange or blue, but black;
the vital passages crossed out,
censored, as in movies,
those bars across
women's breasts. Page one
reveals a diseased lung,
then victory (but whose?).
Page three: a hat, moneylust,
devotion. No neat little-girl-
-to-woman-to-great-poet
unfolding. No photograph
without a veil of slashes.
And though I am angry
and jerk the book away . . .
this, I have learned,
is how she lives: dodging sequence,
applauding herself for slips.
Page four she keeps intact—
an edgy poem with animals.
She's Emily's tiger,
crouched in the grass,
its body sheltered
by ragged, upstanding lines.

Reaction Wood

How composed, your young face.
No evidence of cruelty, my hand over your mouth,
my hand locked around your arm, listen, I tell you
till my fingers ached. Forty days
of heat slamming up against the house.
My angry hand, slapping you,
your thigh, your back. No evidence.
Hardly a whisper
or sign of my voice thrilling
witch, witch, which truthfully
I am afraid, described me.

And somewhere the oak is trimmed,
knicked, irritated by a rude,
burrowing thing. Wire, perhaps.
Inside, molecules erupt.
Reaction wood they call it: cells
in triple growth, dividing,
dividing, covering like a bridge,
like a merciful Chinese fan
until the tree is healed.

Content, one could say, to bear the grudge.

Concubine of the Lowest Rank

She smoothed the sheets, swept the mats.
She lay down and let a thousand gnats
gorge themselves. They flew off drunkenly
like small, blood-filled balloons. Pushy
servant fingers plucked her clothes off
bit by bit. Only one place left
to stash a knife and they checked that
too. A great cleansing wind drove
their footsteps back; a whistle blasted
from the hall and she tried to hum
away her thoughts, force them flat.
She wanted no mind-muddying love
or hate, so when he entered at last
there would be room, plenty of room.

Three Notes from a Chinese Love Manual

1. *THE WHITE TIGER LEAPS*

He jumps from behind, flying like a shard
of glass or maybe cloud. The terror lies
in not knowing which. Too proud
to turn around, you memorize
the light before you, jade, flowers.
You think: I see this, I can
control something. Naked, on all fours,
you bury the desire to run,
imagine his adoring yellow eyes
and claws closed up. And when
he takes you by surprise,
you hang on to your vision
of roses and jewels and falling
light. Quickly he devours it all.

2. *THE FISH INTERLOCK THEIR SCALES*

To succeed, the female inches on top,
a climb against water and grace
with only her limbs supporting her,
sturdy columns. And now what? His map
is exactly reversed and so, useless.
Choose instead which square
of light or dark, how fast
to make him follow, his breath
expectant, restrained. And when
he winces or tries to swim past,
speak vividly of death,
the sameness of pleasure and shame.
He must believe this pretence
and try not to seek forgiveness.

3. *TWO FISH EYE-TO-EYE*

They form a two-part oval
like praying hands. When you pray
you expect God to greet you halfway,
palm-to-palm, soul-to-soul.
The same with your lover, sensual twin.
Try not to fault him his slack skin
or bunched up lip. He simply mirrors
where gravity tugs on your face.
Look in his eye. And if still
you're afraid to be kissed
too deeply and he's not sure
he likes your faults up close,
think of two boats, joyfully spilling
their secrets to lie together like this.

Birth

Excuse me she said and wobbled out alone
not wanting the shame of the others
who proudly announced their time
and then gave birth to untimely
little girls. No one knew, no one discovered
her condition until she pushed him
out, tiny plum seed, uncut diamond
on the damp hay. A boy. Sold
for double the price. Money for the emperor,
happiness for me! *and she danced,*
swinging and jiggling her little package
like a purse. No wonder.
A boy and his mother easily advance.
A girl: two ghosts tied back to back.

Man Drinking a Cup of Coffee

Sometimes when the moon is
simply too full, the ground
dissolves and his house,
so arch in its steel boots,

fills with the flurry of lake.
Murmuring beneath his sand-bagged
basement, it boils into the black
drainage pipe.

He shuffles dry to the kitchen,
gripping his empty cup
my porcelain quarry, he muses,
as he lifts the pitcher high

and the coffee pulls brown legs
together and dives suddenly in:
Venus. Virginia. Ophelia.
Outside, the rain and mourning doves

like purses of wet sand. Imagine
if he lived in a puddle. Clouds
would be huge, murky slippers.
A round black window in the sky

and the women peering in.
The chandelier sways like a
giant udder but, remember,
he refused his mother's breast.

This will make him a saint
of course, a respected leader.
He bolts his coffee and Ophelia
surges down his throat,

her long dark dress spreading
into all his secret places.

Circles, after Emerson

What you said last Saturday
set me thinking. So I yanked down
your house and hammered up my own
on its shaded foundation. Later
someone else came in
with his gritty machinery, *his* plan
for light and incredible wealth.

I put down my drink, watch a ring
of white rot into the wood.
Those timeless ecological arrows!
They bite into everything. For once
I'd like to hold an insignificant leaf,
just a leaf, watch it flutter
for its own sake.

There's the loop of my thirties,
my forties, each decade
with its own little clock.
And the round of my lover's face.
His optimism seemed endless.
Now it's quaint, cute, a small pond.
I spread my arms

like Da Vinci's renaissance man,
probing for what circles me.
Some larger idea, some microscopic thing.
How lucky the plastic jug
that sits and sits in the ravine.
And nobody asks why
or what use it could have

except to hold chlorine.
It rolled and then it stopped.
I too want to stick out
in the soup of nutrients, inedible,

my words worth the argument,
the earth flat, my chair soft.
I love this life.

Star Fish

I like my stars cool, dry
and flat, an infinity
I can fill with flowers and light.

But this fallen,
cheap sort of creature
spits at the afterlife. Its body

grows a lost arm, its arm
a lost body. I've seen them
wrapped about an oyster

like an older sister with a grudge.
She'll choke your secrets out.
From above, it looks like love

so no one interferes. I pry away
its little cups sucking on a clam's
shell, rip them into shreds

like the letter I once got
from a boy who praised too easily.
I wanted to breathe freely.

I want a death I can pity.
Wart, phantom toe, sea star,
is there ever an end to your messy life,

a beach somewhere, where you repent
and the waves forgive
and carry you into the sun?

Her Advice to the Emperor, 1855

"Like crazed horses the two-tongued
strangers advance. Come. Edge closer.
Let me describe swatches of broken
bones, zigzagged skeletons, an odor
of rage and hurry. My voice hums
from your homeland, from half-eaten shells
of houses. The foreigners are coming.
Like locusts they shave the hills.
They strip and forage plains.
Crush and grind and tame,
my darling, their vicious hunger
or my voice will give you no rest.
My voice is the breeze behind your fire.
Breathe fire on them, dragon dearest."

Ideogram

(after Fenollosa)

"Give me a room full of seeds and nails.
Butter, not yellow. Moon, not bright.
Let me work out my problems here
like the cook with her pointed finger.
A philosopher would say: moon, *then* light,
then radiation, cosmos, *and soon he's pale*
from too much thought, lost in one airy
little phrase. I want truth with grass
stains, truth with sticky feet.
The beggarwoman who visited last night—
I praised her for her apples, her fast
walk. She was poor (there's that ladder away)
but I liked her. Instead of bleating I am,
she reached out and grabbed the moon."

Motherly and Auspicious

One morning the Emperor, soothed
by wine and fair weather, rang for his slippers.
And when the Empress came
he waived the usual kowtow, proclaimed:
You are not to do that anymore.
Get up. *She stifled her racing heart, moved,*
as he wished, very close.
Let your hair fall and it veiled
his eyes. Hold my hand
and he wriggled into a shoe. Because you care
for my well-being and nothing else,
you shall be rich, you shall be titled
Motherly and Auspicious. *Then grandly*
he left with one foot bare.

Crossing Guard

Holier than I am
because of where she stands—
opposite the Catholic church
in high heeled boots
and vestments edged with chartreuse.
Or how she stands, so constant,
eyes fixed to traffic, the wide
yellow cross. I
have an appetite for glory,
but I'm looking ahead,
where the road narrows
and there's just a crack
for someone special like me.
She hoists her arm and the giant
recycling truck hisses close,
while children in blazers
skim across, a loose chromatic scale.
No . . . a littered moat.
The end will not be fire or ice.The end
will come in a great tumble
of debris. Crowded into a paperweight,
our sunken motionless city.
Finally, she beckons!
lifting her lime green flare
to bob above the traffic like a duck.
Under the light, she's hardly a body,
a shadowy blip. But that's enough . . .
I'm in first gear, second,
zero to heaven in less than a minute.
I'll bet she never thinks
paradise. And yet,
tapping her heels together,

she pulls herself up like a key.
Suddenly the air before her
shudders, swings open.

Extra Extra

She's dressed to kill,
scarlet off-the-shoulder
minidress, matching sheers
and bangs moussed
like a spray of river
backed up behind a rock.
Her bag's hooked on a pinky
and she swings it,
tight little orbit,
parachuting
maple key. You flash back
to a fall morning
by sheer luck catching
the sudden sexual rain—
a thousand seeds
from one overripe tree.
It had to be
overkill, all that action
for a single coupling
into succulent, condition-red
soil. But now that you
think of it, there's
something extra here too,
an endearing messiness
as she flips her bag
once too often
and it flies smack
into her best
friend's abdomen.
She's blown her cool
but there's wisdom
in losing it too.

Call it instinct?
—this woman knows
in the beginning
life exploded:
a universe, a home
from all that swirling
powder and shadow
and gloss.

Group Photo in the Baby Factory

We gather in our hospital
nightgowns, submitting ourselves
as ideal parents.
We wait for some sign,
a golden chord
before rising.

Above the piano, Schumann's
Soldier's March
and, how odd! ants
masquerading as musical notes.
I see they too
cannot stand the suspense and break
into a chaotic scramble.

What do we do now?
The nurse next door
has turned into a mountain.
Better not ask.
Find some other visual cue.

Someone, for example,
has scattered cherries
on the veneered end tables.
Not even the courtesy
to place them in a bowl . . .
But I notice the guard
has a cherry on his armband,
a cherry pinned to his lapel.

We all grab for one.
Inside, we discover a seed
that resembles a stone.
This will become the child.
Or else it will just be a stone.

The Empress Speaks to Buddha

"I can't imagine life cradled between
give and take, fear and desire.
Will no skeleton hands tug from one side
or the other? I pace your garden
and pigeons scatter though one remains,
his tongue fastened like wire
to seed. Pure animal greed—
he's consumed by it, lost judgement.
Will I too hunger in your gray skin
and your goose down pouch? Or will the light
make everything too even, like the unsmiling
eunuchs I couldn't rouse with a pin?
I like weakness and the flight
back up again. It's defining."

She Buys a Fan

Look at the elders stumble in.
Their honesty leaves them papery skin,
tearing eyes. She buys a dense
coral-pink spray—every utterance
a half secret, gifts she keeps
partly for herself. Her deeper thoughts
are black, swimming
creatures better left clinging
in the dark. Let's quit the requirement
to make our souls transparent.
Lower the blinds, raise our fans
against their outstretched hands.
World, accept some mystery!
In time you will have all of me.

The Empress Receives the Head of a Taiping Rebel

This is the right gift for a poet
who enjoys ordering the sound of water,
who rises late and draws tight
blinds against the advancing sun. She uncovers
the wooden box, her mouth for one second
gaping, resembling his. Oh, how much his expression
contains! The abandon, the sureness, the moment
he stumbled and the sword spread his throat
wide open. To have it all here,
written down! Frozen possibility, like a fruit
that ripens only once in a thousand years.
She caught him in the act of ripening, and tonight,
like a fruit, he'll hang on a tree,
whispering to her of longevity.

The Uniform Quiet of the Next Century

That evening, a discreet little bomb ignited at her dining room table: she praised the latest book but one of her guests disagreed so forcefully her thoughts began to erode. She felt herself swaying, doubting like the insect that drains itself of scarlet before it mimics the sheen of a linden leaf. Soon the whole party exploded, no, imploded, solemnly affirming of course yes yes he's right. She felt dishonest, morally washed out—but this, she reasoned, was the price for advancement: a compression of self to save the self, like the butterfly's paper-thin profile in high sun, like any word recited till it's trivial, absurd, finally new. She nodded *me too,* and gradually the argument settled down, a powdery fall of exhaled breath and nervous hands into their napkins. She rose to fetch the sorbet, spotting on her walk back a lime-green aphid perched on the tip of a mint leaf. She brought two fingers together over its thin life and pressed, hard.

Cautionary Tale, 3 AM

Once there was a scream tumbled out of a car,
planted itself briefly
in our front lawn like a black iris,
swiveled its tongue about, drew police.

I was awake and worried, *cat* or *fight*
and later, *drugs and beer,*
maniac. Pity, I thought,
this was not that kind of street.

And I released the curtain tiebacks
no longer soft, no longer cotton.
Daggers, in fact, though the scream
faded down the hall, nothing more than

rust, lightning, a Dow Jones peak;
merely dusted the back rooms
where the children slept, where the children
sleep. This I'd come to expect

from a demon who likes to lash out,
then fold himself into subtler form—
humidity or shadow or the paring knife's
sudden dive . . . save me from this

elaboration. There was a scream.
I am to blame for everything after.
For the rain I took as blood.
The menace in the flower, its blackness.

Stillborn

She was the accident
born at the edge
of the sun,
snapped off, an ice cold
finger of flame.
I know. I stayed behind.
I watched as she
shed her bloody wrap,
the aluminum calipers.
Watched as she plucked
bead after tiny bead
from their viney
double Helix.

To see her now,
I have to squint.
I close my body eye
like a marksman
and everything turns
clear as reason,
sharp. I see the stain
on her loose silk shirt.
I see the ash, and tumble of
Popeye bones she has
fashioned into a hut.
Tiptoeing towards me
she raises one finger.
She raises a white
and wicked doubt.

Clear Air Turbulence

I never forgot the story—four co-eds
boating too far. When water stilled
and the breeze died, they announced a swim
and one by one jumped into the sea,
quitting their unanchored skiff a
tumble of jokes. And when they'd played enough,
floating careless in the trustworthy light,
the strongest one threaded back to the boat,
bobbing up. Then fluttered and scraped,
but the edge remained above,
riding too high, weightless in the water.
How terrible, that reaching...
Secretly I welcomed the jolt,
coming like the bit of gum that snags
your foot on the pavement, or the cloud
wedge that drops you in shade.
A little terror's good, a little worry
wakes the body double
which is far more courageous
than the shivering bones I live in now.
So on the night my daughter came up from sleep,
legs vibrating like a diving board,
stomach and throat squeezed tight a mockery
of suffocation (what's happening to me? she whined),
I went to meet her. I shook out
tablets, a glass of milk and, good captain,
laid down my voice like an anchor
for both of us. Let's shut the window,
I said. There will be
no foolishness tonight, no
shadows flying from a loose curtain.
No wind passing over our faces like a wave.

The Empress and the Railroad

Some were curious when iron
roads fell across the fields.
She was awake under the wheat
and she trembled. Some called
it magic when iron snakes hung
pole to pole, tied
up the air with their clicking teeth.
She had been singing but fell
silent. Now rust bleeds into everything.
Enemy arms swing, their crosses
like slapdash stars. She loves best
an empty sky, a sleeping plain.
Some feel she should be generous,
open her heart. Let them call her heartless.

The Empress's Dwarf Apricot

At every joint another needle of green.
She prunes to fit the oval
table—new buds, the fleshy main
tuber. Now let the auxiliary root system
take over, furrow deep into black soil.
Its hidden rhizomes are like dangling
tongues, for desire burns low when contained
but burns nevertheless. Prune again
and it turns to concentrate, gunpowder
strong. She staggers up, dizzied
by too much stooping, the rush
of blood to her brain. With her headdress
and sinewy neck, she looks top heavy.
Tiny tree, burdened by its flowers.

Ideogram II

The moon, finding its limit, inches back.
An acorn falls, and so begins
the summer's change of heart. Time,
I'd say, for momentary slack.
Stroke the heel into clay and scribble in
five frozen toes. Draw the line
where they stand, motionless. The eunuchs seem
puzzled and vigorously shake
their heads. They till
the garden but nothing grows. They rattle a bell
and wonder why it doesn't sing.
Lao-tse once asked, who can rake
the muddy water clear? Let it be still,
and it will clear itself.

Hot Water

Moving your hand under the tap,
you're happy to find a simple
chill was the reason
for your worry, and common hunger
scribbled the morning too dark,
the problem unsolvable.
No trouble, no trouble at all.

Outside a man douses his car
with a kettleful.
The door relaxes. Ice cannot
resist, nor cocoa,
nor those cleft pebbles of barley
confessing to fleshiness,
the way character

is nursed out by affliction.
You lower yourself into the tub,
knees like pink bolsters,
breasts whitening eggs.
Is imitation
suicide, as they say? Or Paradise,
that moment of losing

yourself in the other?
First you are separate and mean,
then larger, clouding up, generous,
another thing entirely
like honey sliding off
the spoon, or the teabag
that bleeds, gladly, into its bath.

Villanelle in the Open

Because I was rich, I was sent away empty.
I found my way into the woods and there
my body became a room

the tiny wings deserted—dragonflies, gnats.
I thought my ears would be a draw
but because I was rich, I was sent away empty,

like a narrow ravine. Animals fled
from the edge of me to green safety.
My body had more than enough room

and every moment it gained a little more.
My cord of wood lost its backbone.
(Because I was rich, fire went away empty.)

My bouquet fell. Perhaps my heart too
was only pretending to be a heart,
my body changed into an airless room

by a vacuum engine, some appetite
hard at work fashioning nothing.
Because I was rich, I was sent away empty,
and my body cooled like a shuttered room.

The Empress Calls on the Goddess of Mercy

"God's handmaid is composed of many hands,
wheelspokes testing,
gentle spider legs. A spider touches your skin
before walking there. She wants to know a bit,
to trust. I don't eat meat
to prove my worthiness. I burn candles and sin.
My fingers are stiff. Before praying,
I wait for your kiss. Your glance
relaxes, breaks up my stoniness
like the woman who lifts her daughter
from an ice cold bath.
Oh, hold me to your breast.
Share the poverty, the holiness of the spider
who found a rope to the heavens in herself."

Moon Cakes

Call it stuffing: raisins coated
with flour, nuts, fruit.
Or call it conspiracy, the seeds of revolt.
The cake is just a carrier, a cloak.
The secret, buried inside, takes root
and when the time comes, holds
good women together. For the elders—
baked-in paper, scribbled with a place
and time to banish Moguls
from the North. For the Empress, an SOS
on three beans, painted with white
sugar. Her enemy is an isolated life.
Her enemy is a moonless night
when an outstretched hand appears cut off.

Highway Marker, Route 71 Carrollton

I.

In the corner of one eye,
it floats, green
chip reminding me
May 14, 1988:
            the bus door
demolished, flames sprang up,
children clamoring for breath,
shoving toward the bolted
rear exit with its tiny window,
its modest throat.

The fifth anniversary's
next Friday and someone
has rubber-banded a
Kroger bouquet to the sign's
aluminum post. Crowd
of yellow and pink, those rust
red carnations . . .

            In the kindest
of one mother's dreams,
she saw her little girl
wave from the tip of a human
pyramid, her delighted collapse
into the chaos of wiggling
arms and legs.

A commuter, not a mourner,
I notice on my second
swing by the sharp grade
of neighboring hills. Railroad ties
pinned like barrettes
hold back the soil
from its easy slide down.

To mourn
is to hover, to cling tightly
like a pressure garment.

II.

Suppose, instead of quiet,
we drove into the accident itself,
played over and over
like museum movies
of vanished Indian tribes?
Suppose the highway saved
these events, collected them,
its shoulders jammed, pavement
impassable?

Some believe too much sorrow
barricades the soul
of the lost one. After time,
the gate snaps open again,
and the soul steps out,
releasing its silken flood
of images.

In the kindest of one
father's dreams, he saw seared
grooves on his daughter's skin
change to faint imprints,
as if all this time she had
only been napping, her cheek pushed
against the candlewick spread.

Somewhere,
not far, twenty-four white crosses
float above the shifty soil.
They stand, I have heard,
outside the flare of halogens,
beyond the highway which
presses into the mountains
like an iron bar.

Water House, Shakertown

The sky is a cruel door
that opens easy
for smoke and scent,

swings wide for chiffon
or a mimosa leaf,
but not for me.

I want you, it says
but only a little.
What a tease—

skin made for shedding
all chipped yellow clapboard
and sway backed roof

while inside, the skeleton's
resolute, brick after ruddy
brick, and cool, like

tombstone. I have seen it all:
Sister Ann with her stolen
hour of idleness.

Farmers and trustees
and the sweatered tourists
shuffling up

their money's worth.
Some say satisfaction
is fleeting.

I find it long and tedious.
I wish to live precariously
like a beaded curtain,

a sweater or a rug
woven with sequins
the most common light

splinters into
a thousand speedy beams.
Mine is a patient angel,

old-fashioned, reticent.
Make way for the image
of God, she sighs

as the rain falls and the wind
darts forward; then as usual
she reconsiders.

Oval

I understand. Harmony. And wheels
of all sizes fell from the sky.
Hulahoops, coins, pearls, tires.

I made a nest in one and lived happily.
And also—my face was round!
But really, it's oval, lop-sided,

the forehead peaked, jaw pointed, no cheekbones
to speak of. Why oval?
An oval's unsettling, like a racetrack

or the lope of planets about the sun.
Suppose God is like the sun—
and cannot keep a perfect hold

on all his followers. So he lets us
come and go, wobble and burn.
Look at Mars, said Kepler, despairing.

Indeed, if God wanted loyal children
why did he give me such a short fuse,
a brain that questions everything?

Why did he make my face oval,
like the gem on my mother's hand
which pokes uncomfortably into her flesh?

Last Request

"The dead cannot shout so let me
show you the way to honor.
Build me a paper house crammed with money,
paper lutes, bells, jugglers.
Burn them all quickly. Smoke
is a kind of heavenly translator.
I cannot choke.
I will be without breath, my heart
vacant. So fill up that cardboard flask
and double my portion of rice.
In return, I'll bless your marriage bed.
Don't hesitate to ask
for more. Our need connects us.
It's freedom I dread."

The Dying Empress

No surprise. A nearly perfect guess.
They roll her body, opal-fingered, in,
gauze draped like a tent
just as her breath begins to digress.
Old woman, she is spun
of planets and gases and light bent
from eons back. Palace mothers
cup their pale hands, thinking
of their young, the rasp
sucking in the dark. Very soon
the moon will turn, her light waver.
Above, a small rectangular window, just opening.
She laughs and reaches one last
time into space. Release the black balloon.

Bisecting a Water Lily

Choose the lily for the knife can slice
not one, but five ways like a star.

Pull back the stamens from their ring
about the ovary. Let them fall,

filament by filament into the petal's
lemon canoe. Puncture stigma and style

then finally the ovules in their ripe casing.
Did you find it cruel, savoring each miniature half,

watching it wilt as the stain settled on your hand?
Did you pray for a hormone, the merciful, numbing kind?

Call it longing, or balance, or compensation,
but I believe every thing completes itself

even in detachment. The half becomes whole again,
the missing piece ghosted like the blue

that drains from a clipped chicory, or soup
tipped to the downside of a bowl. We are,

you recently said, farther apart than ever,
and threw me a withered look. But I believe for change

it takes this collapse of will.
Even a broken lily scatters pollen,

seeds to the swampy floor. We wade out
to gather more. The stream heals up behind us.

Snow Melt

When the snow fell, adding its weight
sympathetically, layer by layer,

when the housekeeper finally hushed
her argument with your temper,

you settled back quietly,
happily insulated. The end, you imagined,

had arrived, like that point in a blizzard
when you give up trying to phone,

trying to scrape the windows of their ice.
But now the air is heating up. Cars pare down

to their teenage shape and telephone poles
are suddenly bony and brown as calf legs.

You're moving backwards in time, light
bouncing and ricocheting like pinballs.

Your mother steps out of the dark,
her white coat melting in a puddle at her feet.

You feel your little sister's pinch
and there are the muffins you ate and then

the hunger for them. The room sizzles with electricity,
flashes of information like a gust

of aspen leaves. Finally you are whisked away,
consoled with your freedom,

lifted from your birth like a vapor
forgetting its swirl of silver bubbles.

I Go Back

Back into longing and expectation
and my body again plumps up.
I had worn it with indifference.

I go back into grief, to the beached
dolphin I touched
with just two fingers,

to the shoestring, radio antenna,
fishing line I left hanging.
Hope finally meets its little fish,

finds it smaller than expected.
I go back into sunsuits, terrycloth,
my skin fiery underneath,

back when the wanting was richer
than anything I own,
when my wrist bones floated

and my skull was unlocked.
When pinpricks on the horizon
blossomed into sailboats

and I memorized their names.
Yes, I go back into longing,
attention, to precision,

with my vagueness and my years
and my sarcasm like water
rushing into a hole in the sand.

Notes: Sonnets to the Last Empress

In the opening sequences of Bertolucci's film, *The Last Emperor,* the esteemed T'zu-hsi, Empress Dowager, lies on her deathbed—limbs straightened, face towards the south, a black pearl in her mouth to keep her soul from escaping. After ruling for forty-six years, she rallies briefly to appoint the two-year-old grandson of a favorite general—ritual, but not blood heir to her throne. P'u-i reigns a scant three years before the Imperialist system collapses, making way for Communist rule.

This small, potent scene was a perfect poetic trigger for me, but my curiosity tilted backwards in time, not forwards like the film. It was the last Empress who captivated, a woman balanced on the edge of transformation: powerlessness into power, then back again, birth into death into rebirth— the constantly shifting plane Tibetans call "bardo."

The series combines narrative with impressionistic pieces and adheres only loosely to historical fact. It is a fact, however, that T'zu-hsi was born a middle-class Manchurian, entered the Imperial Palace as a fifth-place concubine, then rose quickly through the ranks by birthing a son as heir to the Emperor's throne. When the Emperor's health declined, T'zu-hsi became Empress at the age of 26. Her reign was marked with turmoil, including internal rebellions; threats from the British, French, Japanese, and Russians; as well as the premature death of her son from smallpox. Despite all this, the Empress held on until 1908. The Imperial system collapsed in 1912.

The *"Three Notes from a Chinese Love Manual"* are drawn from several handbooks of erotic lore—*The Art of the Bedchamber, Important Guidelines of the Jade Room,* etc. They describe various sexual positions.

"Her Advice to the Emperor, 1855"—Refers to one year during the Taiping Rebellions.

"Motherly and Auspicious"—Just two of the sixteen titles the Empress received. Each title involved an increase in status, respect, and salary.

"Last Request"—Upon the Empress's death, paper models of soldiers, servants, clothes, and money were burned in the belief that these things would pass on to her in the afterlife, the "World of Shadows."

SARAH GORHAM is a poet and publisher who currently resides in Louisville, Kentucky. She received an MFA from the University of Iowa in 1978 and a BA in 1976 from Antioch College.

Her first full-length collection of poems, *Don't Go Back to Sleep,* was published by Galileo Press in 1989.

Gorham's poems have been published widely in such magazines as *Poetry, The Nation, Antaeus, Grand Street, The Kenyon Review, Ohio Review, Missouri Review, Ploughshares,* and *Poetry Northwest,* where in 1990 she won the Carolyn Kizer Award. Other awards include grants and fellowships from The Kentucky State Arts Council, The Kentucky Foundation for Women, The Delaware State Arts Council, The Connecticut Commission on the Arts, Yaddo, and MacDowell. In 1983, she received the Gertrude Claytor Prize from the Poetry Society of America.

In March 1994, Gorham founded Sarabande Books, Inc., a small press devoted to the publication of poetry and short fiction.

Gorham is the wife of poet Jeffrey Skinner and the mother of two daughters, Laura and Bonnie. They live in a 1907 beige clapboard house with one rabbit, one bird, a dog named Emma, and a fairly average amount of chaos.